Nature Upclose

A Mealworm's Life

Written and Illustrated by John Himmelman

Children's Press®
A Division of Grolier Publishing

New York London Hong Kong Sydney
Danbury, Connecticut

For all you insect lovers!

Library of Congress Cataloging-in-Publication Data

Himmelman, John
A mealworm's life / written and illustrated by John Himmelman.
    p. cm. — (Nature upclose)
    Summary: Describes the daily activities and life cycle of a
mealworm beetle.
    ISBN 0-516-22261-9 (lib. bdg.)   0-516-27286-1 (pbk.)
    1. Mealworms—Life cycles—Juvenile literature. [1. Meal-
worms.] I. Title
QL596.T2 H56 2001
595.76'9—dc21   00-055574
                                           CIP

Visit Children's Press® on the Internet at:
http://publishing.grolier.com

GROLIER
PUBLISHING   1 2 3 4 5 6 7 8 9 10 R 10 09 08 07 06 05 04 03 02 01

Yellow Mealworm
Tenebrio molitar

Many teachers keep mealworms in their class-rooms. They are easy to raise, and children enjoy watching them grow and change. Meal-worms eat all kinds of grains, so you might find them in flour, chicken feed, or breakfast cereal.

As a mealworm grows, it may shed its hard outer exoskeleton as many as twenty times. When the mealworm becomes a pupa, it cannot move. For about two weeks, all kinds of changes happen inside the hard case that sur-rounds the pupa. Then an adult beetle emerges.

At first, the beetle is very pale, but soon it grows darker. Some people call mealworm beetles "darkling beetles." They eat the same kinds of food as young mealworms, so you may see them together. Some people think that mealworm beetles cannot fly, but they can—especially if they are attracted by a light.

Mealworm beetles live for about three months. They prefer dark, humid places and often live in the food they eat.

On a warm spring evening, a mealworm beetle spots a pile of grain in the corner of a shed.

She lays her eggs in the grain.

A week later, a young mealworm crawls out of her egg.

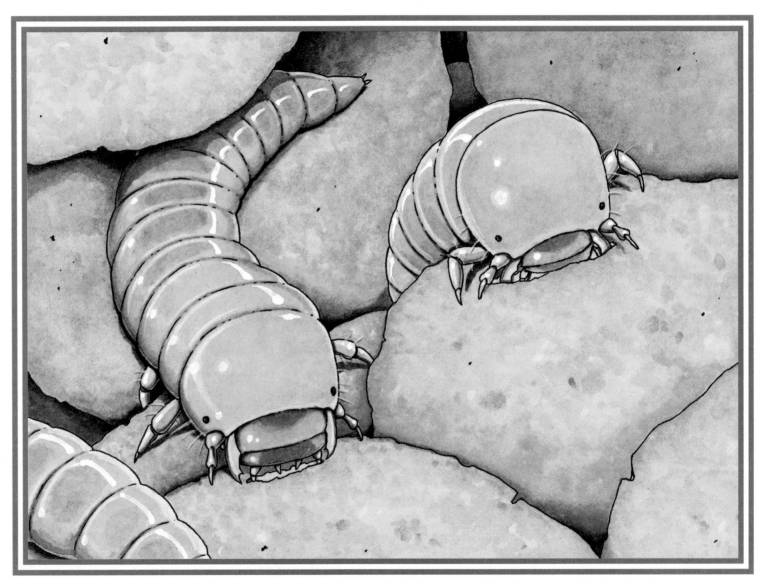

Other mealworms *hatch* too. They spend most of their time eating.

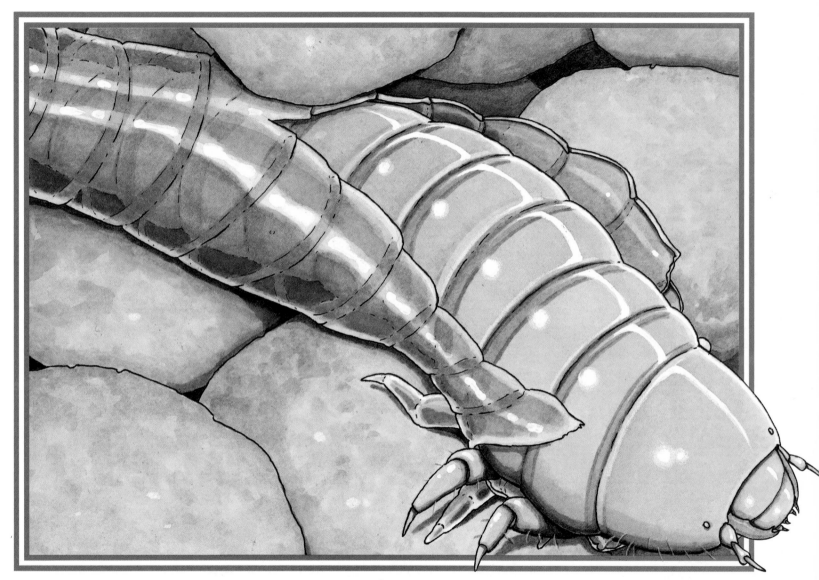

Soon the mealworm is too big for her skin. She sheds her *exoskeleton*.

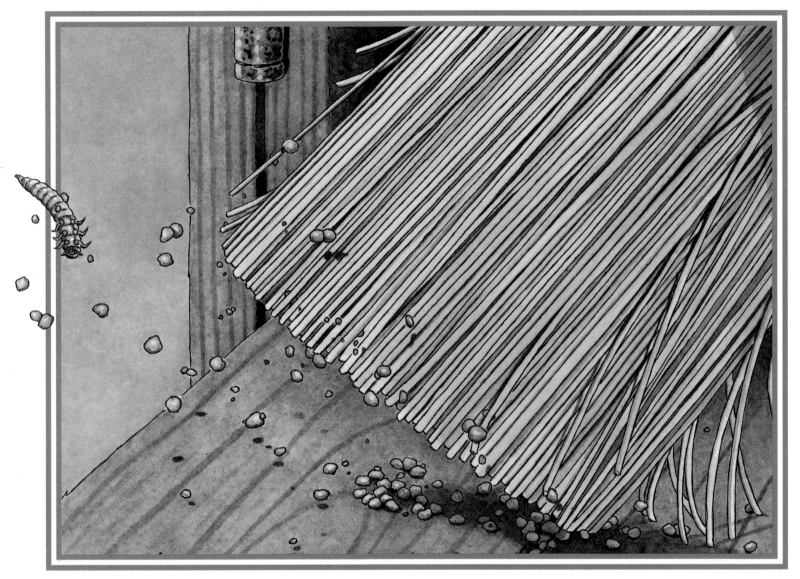

On a sunny summer morning, the mealworm is swept outside.

She wanders into a chicken coop and spots some food on the ground.

It is a dangerous place to have a meal! But the chicken doesn't notice her.

In the autumn, the mealworm leaves the chicken coop to find more food.

The mealworm returns to the shed where she hatched.

She climbs into an open bag of grain.

It is the perfect place to spend the long, cold winter.

When spring arrives, the mealworm changes into a *pupa*.

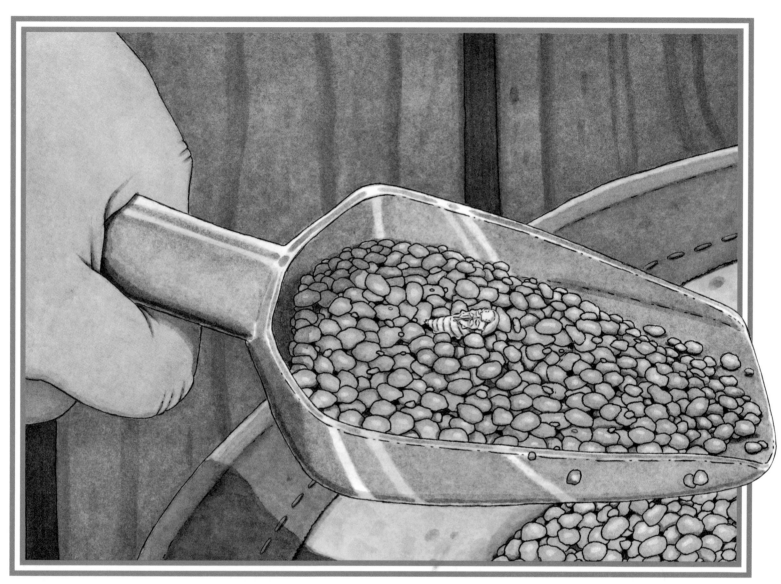

A person scoops up some grain—and the pupa!

Will the chicken eat her?

The chicken does not see the pupa. When the pupa turns into an adult beetle, she can escape.

The mealworm beetle hides from the daylight under the chicken's water dish.

As the beetle grows, her body gets darker. She leaves her hiding place to search for food.

All summer long, the beetle eats while the chicken sleeps.
Sometimes she shares a meal with a *white-footed mouse.*

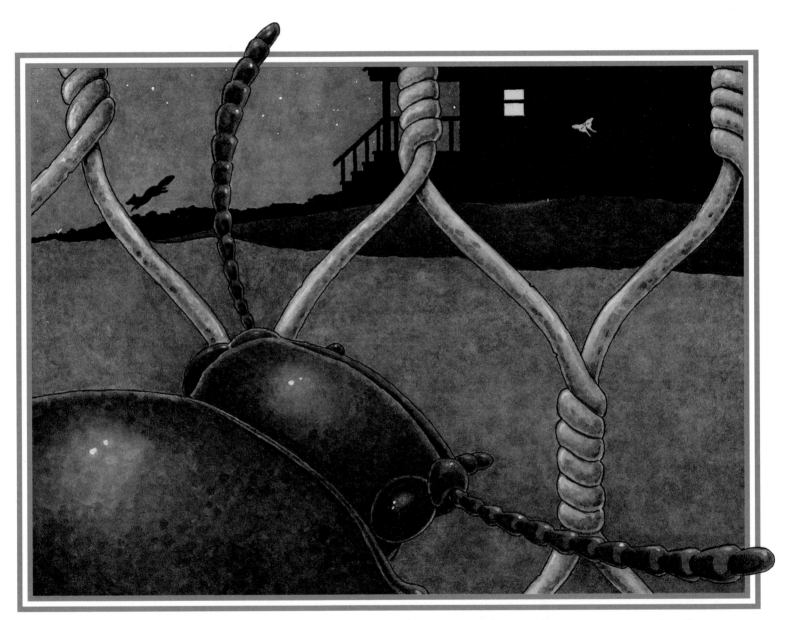

On a cool autumn night, the mealworm beetle spots a light in the distance.

She flies toward the light. It is coming from a house.

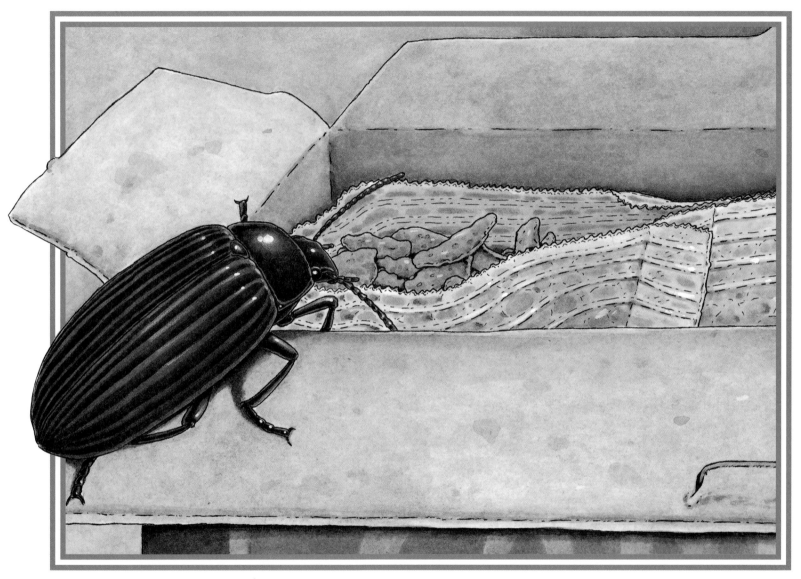

The beetle crawls through a window and finds a box of cereal.

In the morning, a child pours the cereal—and the beetle—into a bowl.

But the beetle is not there for long! The child dumps her out.

Later that evening, the mealworm beetle returns to the shed.
That is where she will spend the winter.

In the spring, another mealworm beetle joins her.

After they mate, she lays her eggs.

She will not live to see another spring, but her *offspring* will.

Words You Know

exoskeleton—the hard outer covering of insects and some other animals

hatch—to break out of an egg

offspring—the young of a plant or animal. Human offspring are called children.

pupa—the second stage of a mealworm's life

white-footed mouse—a small mouse common in fields and wooded areas

About the Author

John Himmelman is a naturalist who enjoys turning over dead logs, crawling through grass, kneeling over puddles, and gazing at the sky. His greatest joy is sharing these experiences with others. He has written or illustrated more than fifty books for children, including *Ibis: A True Whale Story, Wanted: Perfect Parents,* and *J.J. Versus the Babysitter.*

His books have received honors, such as CBC/NSTA Outstanding Science Trade Book for Children, Pick of the List, Book of the Month, JLG Selection, and the ABC Award. Some of the illustrations he has created for the Nature Upclose series were featured at an exhibit at Yale University's Peabody Museum of Natural History in New Haven, Connecticut. John lives in Killingworth, Connecticut, with his wife, Betsy, who is an art teacher. They have two children, Jeff and Liz.